Aging in Place

Calliope Chapbook Series

Lynn Aprill

This collection of poems is a human-made work of imagination. No part of this book may be reproduced, distributed, or transmitted in any form or by any means without written permission of the publisher, except in the case of brief quotations used in a review of the book.

Aging in Place
© Lynn Aprill, 2025
All rights reserved.

ISBN: 978-1-952526-25-1

Published in the United States
as a part of
Calliope Chapbook Series,
a collaborative project with
Lakeland University's Literary Publishing class:
Editors: Madeleine Wattenberg, Assistant Professor,
Sarah Stege, Miranda Arnold, and Leanna Jankowski

Water's Edge Press LLC
Tucson, Arizona

Cover image licensed through Shutterstock
Cover and book design by Water's Edge Press LLC

NO AI TRAINING: Without in any way limiting the author's and publisher's exclusive rights under copyright, any use of this publication to "train" generative artificial intelligence (AI) technologies to generate text is expressly prohibited. The author reserves all rights to license uses of this work for generative AI training and development of machine learning language models.

I
A Boomer at 60

YMCA—The Women

When they see your unfamiliar face,
they make a point of gliding over
through the chlorinated water,

sagging breasts buoyant once again,
apron bellies cinched into
full-body slimming slender suits,

asking your name, inviting you
to coffee or maybe kayaking
if that's your thing, sharing

sourdough starter or a spare bra
if you happen to have forgotten yours
when you packed your bag this morning.

They plan group lunches, put out
sympathy cards when another one
loses a spouse. Their faces surface again

at Sunday services or are resurrected
from the cubicles and classrooms
that you've recently left behind.

You failed to notice them before,
but now your first job upon retirement
is to find them, to become them.

Things I've lost so far: a zuihitsu

✓ my phone

✓ that one book, you know, the one with the bird on the cover

✓ friends

✓ the ability to drive just about anyplace that isn't routine without the crutch of the GPS on my phone

    ✓ my phone

✓ the recipe for porcupine meatballs in the pressure-cooker cookbook, but then I find the recipe—two pounds of hamburger, two tablespoons of dried onion, two teaspoons of salt, a half teaspoon of pepper, one cup of rice—form the mixture into balls and drop them in the pressure cooker into which I've tipped one quart of tomato soup from my basement canning cellar
    I serve the porcupine meatballs for dinner
    They taste like my childhood

✓ my childhood

✓ the ability to drive back home without referring to the GPS on my phone after arriving someplace with the help of the GPS on my phone

    ✓ my phone

✓ the word for that card with my name and my address and information about myself that I hand to people who want to know who I am

✓ who you are

Fearless

Cleaning, I find us fresh-faced
in Polaroids, posing tough

with cigarettes and cups of PBR,
arms looped casually over necks,

middle fingers aloft. We dared
the lens to capture us any other way.

All the things we didn't know—
who would face the first loss

of parent spouse child sibling,
who would go to war,

who would stay together,
who would drift apart—

are now writ large in laugh lines
and silver streaks and knees

that protest when we try to stand
and empty chairs.

The Assignment

In the writing workshop, you're charged with writing an opening sentence in a new style, so you choose "Second Person Adventure Story" and for no good reason you imagine a parachute and construct the following sentence: "As you check your packed parachute one final time, you wonder again if it's too late to beg off, but your best friend's eager, terrified smile convinces you that it's not the craziest thing in the world, or the hardest—sitting with her through chemo and watching her hair fall out and praying to a god you didn't quite believe in not to take her had been agony—this would be a piece of cake," and then you wonder where that sentence came from and why you started with a parachute and you had no idea it would suddenly become a sentence about two friends and cancer, because it *was* agony to watch her believe it was in remission only to have it reappear on another scan (and she was only stage 2 when they caught it and no one is supposed to die of stage 2 cancer) and even though you would not have jumped out of a perfectly good plane with her, you bitterly regret that you could have planned a trip to Ireland together and no matter how many candles you light for her in foreign chapels, you will never forget that you didn't.

Abecedarian for a Doctor's Advice on Menopause

A woman might expect to experience:
Brain fog
Changes in body odor [*reminiscent of my teenage years*]
Dry, itchy skin
Electric shocks [*as a precursor to*]
Flashes [*hot and cold*]
Gum problems [*as in receding*]
Headaches [*tension and migraine*]
Insomnia
Joint pain [*a sudden desire to own a*]
Kayak
Low self-esteem
Mood swings
Night sweats [*with subsequent changes of bedding*]
Osteoporosis
Palpitations [*as of the heart*] [*an increased longing for*]s
Quaint villages [*with quirky coffee shops and pottery studios*]
Reduced sex drive [*Sure, it's ALWAYS the woman*]
Sleep disturbances
Trouble judging distances   [*Seriously?*]
UTIs
Vomiting
Weight gain [*Enough, already!*] Take a
Xanax   [*and calm down?*]
You'll find your
Zen again [*So, essentially, it's all in my head, right?*]

Ode to the Wandering Uterus

For centuries, they believed
that only women could suffer
from hysteria,

> *hystera* being Greek
> for womb, for you,
> O Wandering Uterus,

>> stalking the body
>> like a midnight panther
>> hungry for semen.

If I contracted a cough,
it was you, dear Uterus,
caught in my throat;

> if chest pains, you had settled
> between my ribs, peering
> through the bones,

> biding your time.
> The Egyptians would "move" you
> with pleasing scents

or noxious fumes
to chase you back
to your pelvic home.

The Greeks?
Their answer to everything
was sex—

       fill you up with new life
       and the hysteria will cease,
       or so was the prevailing notion.

As you approached menopause,
poor aging Uterus,
Victorian doctors advised against:

       reading novels,
       going to parties,
       dancing.

             At half a century, instability
             and animal madness
             were considered inevitable.

Only much later, attention moved to the brain,
and you, sweet pulsating Uterus,
were left to your own devices.

Farmer Wants a Wife™: My Boomer Pitch

To begin, I'd stop trotting out
the Gen Z princesses
and Midwest daddy's girls

greeting the new farm day
in peep-toe wedges
and mini crop tops,

ready to stab the competition
with a conveniently packed
stiletto. Instead,

let's make this
a marriage tournament
appropriate to the venue,

testing which prospective Mrs.
can dash to the garden,
pick and can

a dozen quarts of green beans,
wring the neck of the slowest chicken
and turn it into potpie or stew,

chase down the errant calf,
race to finish mowing the lawn
before the next storm,

and fall across
the finish line
of his bed,

exhausted
(but not
too exhausted)—

an agricultural *Squid Game*
where the winner
gets the rock.

That's how you find the farmer a wife.

Role Model

I'm fully aware
that I fucked up my kids

because "body positivity"
wasn't even a thing back then,

when I tried every diet,
every gimmick, every

back-of-the-magazine tip
and trick to lose the belly

and gain the thigh gap.
And yet—here we are again.

So even while my daughter
is congratulating me

for loving my bountiful body
and embracing my Rubenesque curves,

underneath this too too solid flesh,
I'm still searching for an answer

and the cookie jar is empty
and so is the chip bag.

I'M FINE

I'm becoming increasingly aware of a
muffled wail that is rising
from beneath my left kidney,
infiltrating my spinal column, and
nesting at the base of my throat. I
envy Munch his *Scream*.

Foreboding Joy

I've been known . . .

>to shake my sleeping children
>just to make sure they're still breathing;
>
>to write out my last wishes
>as part of my vacation preparation;
>
>to sit far from the cliff edge
>after traveling a lifetime to see the view;
>
>to trust simultaneously
>in the best and the worst of life.

Can one be Pollyanna *and* Eeyore?
Now I have a name

(thanks to Brené Brown)
for this Janus malady,

so next time I get a raise
or publish a poem,

I'll lean into the joy and not think
about the Mack Truck

which may cross my path
on the way home.

Grandson: a sijo

I hold you on my shoulder,
    your small body draped across me.
I inhale your infant scent
    of milk and sweat, powder and sleep.
Bottle it, so I can carry you with me
    when I leave you.

Inheritance: a villanelle

I ask where it hurts, she says, *Everywhere.*
Half asleep, just out of her restless bed,
the pains of age, her growing nightmare.

Exhausted, she meets each new day aware
that waking will not bring relief, instead
when asked where it hurts, she says, *Everywhere.*

She navigates her perilous world with care;
the slightest tumble could end in bloodshed,
concussion, elder care—her worst nightmare.

Each time I visit, I send up a prayer,
but most days, I find her eyes filled with dread.
I ask where it hurts, she says, *Everywhere.*

My own dreams are shattered by the flare
of sleeping limbs, the ache and tingling spreads,
the pains of age becoming *my* nightmare.

Bleary-eyed from lack of sleep, I swear
to bury my discomfort; instead,
I hold my tongue. It hurts everywhere
as pains of age become our shared nightmare.

II

The Silent Generation Ages in Place

The Reimagined Home Mausoleum

Dear Silent Generation,
Let us sell you a dream:
to work yourselves into stooped backs
and arthritic fingers with which to clutch
your homes about your aging bones.

Once the mortgage is finally paid off,
we'll grant your final wish, to die
in this house of pole lamp and La-Z-Boy,
Pyrex and macramé—hallowed shrine
to work-life balance gone awry.

Maybe Tomorrow

He never lost the need
for a nice suit. Even now,

decades into retirement, he rises
each morning, showers and shaves

with a straight razor and shaving soap
lathered in a wooden bowl

with a wood-handled brush, sliding
the thin blade across each cheek.

Next, he pulls on undershorts
and a strap T-shirt, the kind

the young folks call a "wifebeater"—
What a name!—and reaches

into his closet for a clean suit.
He hasn't gained a pound

since he retired, but still
he visits Saul once a year

(or now, Saul's son) and is measured
for a new suit. He has his routine,

shuffling down his street to caffeinate
at the Bump & Grind on the corner,

wandering into the library to scan
The Times, sitting in the park

on nice days to dog-watch
and reminisce about his Jack Russell,

Pete, gone three years now.
Lunch at Ella's Deli, an afternoon

at the Senior Center for bingo
or a game of chess with Ed—

What a blowhard!—and the slow shuffle
home. A can of soup during *Jeopardy*,

a long dive into the latest Michael Connelly,
and the day is done. Tonight, again, he stands

in front of the bedroom mirror, framed
by the pink wallpaper that Judy spent

one whole weekend putting up,
now faded to the blush

on her 18-year-old cheeks
in the long long ago. He kisses

his palm, presses it to the glass—
I'll see you soon, sweetheart.

Maybe tomorrow. Maybe so.

Circus

In the hospital, your dad
tells a joke—*I can read palms*—
to one nurse after another.

"You can?" They stretch a hand,
he grasps and traces a line here,
another long line. "What does it mean?"

*I don't know, but it sure was nice
to hold your hand.* A laugh,
a blush, a pulling back.

The stroke rehab ward is full
of 80-year-old men who keep
these poor girls on their toes—

medical magicians appearing
in room after room, juggling
lunch trays, positioning urinals,

listening to the men talk
farming over the drone
of *The Young and the Restless*

on the lobby TV.
When they move your dad
to the nursing home for rehab,

the jokes stop—the show's over.
Now he stares at his own palm,
hoping to learn how long he'll be here.

Not Another Day at Camp

The first day
is always the hardest:

The room is too small.
And dark.

And there are two beds—
will I have a roommate?

My first meal was tuna salad—
You KNOW I hate mayonnaise!

The bed is too hard.
And there's no phone??!!

I'm so far from the cafeteria,
I'll never make it there in time!

There's no chair in the room.
I don't know anyone.

Do you have to go?
I cry whenever you leave.

I'm sorry, Dad, I know—
we'll be back tomorrow.

On Finding My Father's Medication Has Run Out

Today, I play insurance roulette,
clutch the old phone cord like the arm
of a penny slot, pray to see

Two days, two days, two days
come up in the pay line.
That's all he needs

to move up his prescription,
so I explain to one disembodied voice after another,
people I will never meet, and try to remain calm:

Yes, Amy, we just need the prescription filled today;
Absolutely, John, his doctor has approved it,
my voice a firstborn child stamping

her sneakered feet. Instead
we come up lemons, admit defeat,
pay out of pocket for three pills

to bridge the gap until Friday.
Today, I learn my mother has
six bottles of the same medication

in two different dosages.
I march my poker face
into the pharmacy,

lay my bottles on the counter, explain
how we're going to fix the situation.
I do not blink . . .

Three cherries, baby!
The pharmacy takes back
half of the pills,

processes the return,
and I pocket the cash.
I know when to walk away.

Appeal

She lifts a hand, smooths
wet cloth over thin skin, strokes
long limbs as he reclines,

bedridden, aneurysm victim
and father of a
former classmate. Once

a lawyer, his mind now a file
empty of jurisprudence
and the faces of his family.

She wrings the cloth, proceeds
cautiously to navigate the caldera
of missing skull, moves

to his face, cheeks bristled
as an old brush, pale lips
intent on whispering

shocking obscenities,
his only oral argument now.
After his shave and shine,

he's ready to be recognized,
his family waiting in the hall.
She finishes her tasks

with this eleventh-hour plea—
that he should suddenly
go mute.

Nursing Shortage

In a room
on the cardiac floor,
one patient watches

circus animals cavorting
above her door, holds conversations
with long-dead friends,

is so pumped
full of medication
that she's unrecognizable.

In a room
on the cardiac floor,
this patient thinks

she is eating, bringing
her empty hand
to her open mouth,

where you slip
the loaded spoon,
like a mother robin

tending to her chick,
praying the doctor
will concentrate on

keeping her alive,
not "making her
comfortable."

In a room
on the cardiac floor,
this patient—a fall risk

hopped up on drugs
to keep her compliant—
is propped in a chair

without restraints
while the nurses step
to the desk for a consult.

In a room
on the cardiac floor,
this patient tries to stand,

and instead splits her skull
on the unyielding floor, takes
ten stitches, a fractured orbit,

and a shiner worthy
of a heavyweight round
with her to the nursing home.

In a room
on the cardiac floor,
they wait to find out

if actions have consequences.

Superstitious

My aunt mentions the "grandchild scam"—
Hi, Grandma, don't you recognize my voice?

Ninety, childless, she's far too savvy for their scheme.
Yet, her kitchen table creaks under the weight

of dozens of charity letters, thirty-two free calendars,
ten dream catchers from tribal schools, pleas

for cash—*just a dollar, just pennies a day*—
and we cannot convince her to toss them.

Instead, she sends thirteen donations,
walks around every ladder, hangs

horseshoes right-side up, wraps chains
around her umbrellas so they don't pop open

indoors. There is salt on the floor, tossed
over a left shoulder to blind the devil.

If dementia were a poem,

it would be a found poem—
random words gathered
from scribbled notes
on old envelopes.

Caught

Today, your conversations
skip like a scratched record,
and you recite again and again

the same facts, the same events,
the same details, wishing
he could catch the salient points

and hold them close to his chest
like so many caught softballs,
to turn over later and remember—

Oh, yes, we discussed in-home care;
Of course I took my medication already;
You'll be back on Tuesday, isn't that right?—

but those softballs are soap bubbles
bursting nearly as soon as they're blown,
nothing sticks but a hazy residue.

Melancholy

Two weeks before opening day,
ice still seals the lake,
protecting the fertile trout

from snapping poles and dangling lines.
The knocking of the woodpecker
jackhammers across the lake.

A blue jay lands on the bottom branch,
drops like a stone to the ground,
pecks for his breakfast.

Disgruntled geese
honk their displeasure
at failing to find open water.

In the chilly morning air,
a loon calls across the expanse,
hoping to lure a mate.

On a morning such as this,
you take your final leave of us.
A distant train rumbles on.

Epilogue

For My Daughter

In one children's book
a baby bird asks
every kind of animal

Are you my mother?
This is a question
I never have to ask—

the phantom of my mother's face
is found in every mirror,
my brain is an echo chamber

where my mother's voice resonates.
Some days, this is a question
that my mother cannot answer.

In which tomorrow, my Little Bird,
will I sit with you, wondering
who *your* mother was?

Acknowledgements

Many thanks to the editors of the publications in which some of these poems have appeared, sometimes in different forms:

"Abecedarian for a Doctor's Advice on Menopause." *Instant Noodles*, Devil's Party Press, December 2022.

"The Assignment." First place, "Regrets" category, Poets & Patrons 2024 Poetry Contest.

"The Farmer Wants a Wife: My Network Pitch." *The Broken City*, Summer 2024 edition, Issue 34.

"Heartache" (AKA "If dementia were a poem"). Third Honorable Mention, "Free Verse" Category, Poets & Patrons 66th Chicagoland Poetry Contest, 2022.

"Maybe Tomorrow." *Older Lifespan*, Pure Slush, Vol. 11, 2024.

"Ode to the Wandering Uterus." Third place, Wisconsin Writers Association Jade Ring Contest, Poetry category, 2024.

"Superstitious." Second Honorable Mention, "Miniature" category, Poets & Patrons 2024 Poetry Contest.

With Many Thanks

To my Southampton crew: Wendy, Kathryn, Sara, John, and Willie. None of this exists without you. You make me a better writer every time we meet.

To my awesome sibs Denise, Doug, and Scott and my kids Ben, Mary, Marissa, Josh—my eternal cheerleaders.

To Dale, at home with the dogs keeping the homefires burning until I'm done gallivanting again.

About the Author

Lynn Aprill is an award-winning poet and retired educator whose work has appeared in *Creative Wisconsin*, *Copperfield Review Quarterly*, *Quartet Journal*, *Willows Wept Review*, *Ekphrastic Review*, and others. She is currently an MFA candidate with an emphasis in poetry at Lindenwood University in St. Charles, MO. *Channeling Matriarchs*, her first chapbook with Finishing Line Press, was published in August 2021. She resides with her husband and various dogs on 40 acres in Northeast Wisconsin.

Her work can be found at lynnaprill.weebly.com.

www.ingramcontent.com/pod-product-compliance
Lightning Source LLC
Chambersburg PA
CBHW030534080526
44586CB00011B/431